Deepest Thoughts

SO DEEP
THEY SQUEAK

Jack Handey

HYPERION
NEW YORK

Text design by Carla Weise/Levavi & Levavi, Inc.

Library of Congress Cataloging-in Publication Data
Handey, Jack
    Deepest Thoughts: so deep they squeak / Jack Handey.–1st ed.
        p. cm.
    Based on Saturday night live.
    ISBN 0-7868-8044-9
    1. American wit and humor. I. Saturday night live (Television program)
II. Title
PN6162.H266 1994
818' .5402—dc20   94-18060
                                           CIP

First Edition
10   9   8   7   6   5   4   3   2   1

To Marta?

SPECIAL THANKS TO: Spike Feresten; John Fortenberry and Melissa Christopher; Tom Gammill; Christopher and Maria Hart; Lori Jo Hoekstra; Pat Marble; Ian Maxtone-Graham; George Meyer; Lorne Michaels; William, Linda, Ben and Jesse Novak; Max Pross and Mira Velimirovíc; Maria Semple; Christine Zander; Becky Sue Epstein; and Vickie Warr. You too, Mark Nutter.

SPECIAL THANKS ALSO TO: my agent, Jim Trupin; my editor, Leslie Wells; and most especially my wife, Marta Chavez Handey.

I CAN PICTURE in my mind a world without war, a world without hate. And I can picture us attacking that world, because they'd never expect it.

I HOPE some animal never bores a hole in my head and lays its eggs in my brain, because later you might think you're having a good idea but it's just eggs hatching.

$\mathcal{W}$HENEVER YOU read a good book, it's like the author is right there, in the room, talking to you, which is why I don't like to read good books.

*W*HAT IS IT about a beautiful sunny afternoon, with the birds singing and the wind rustling through the leaves, that makes you want to get drunk. And after you're real drunk, maybe go down to the public park and stagger around and ask people for money, and then lay down and go to sleep.

*I*NSTEAD OF A trap door, what about a trap window? The guy looks out it, and if he leans too far, he falls out. Wait. I guess that's like a regular window.

*D*URING THE Middle Ages, probably one of the biggest mistakes was not putting on your armor because you were "just going down to the corner."

*I*f your kid makes one of those little homemade guitars out of a cigar box and rubber bands, don't let him just play it once or twice and then throw it away. Make him practice on it, every day, for about three hours a day. Later, he'll thank you.

*I*F I EVER get real rich, I hope I'm not real mean to poor people, like I am now.

$\mathcal{W}$HEN I found the skull in the woods, the first thing I did was call the police. But then I got curious about it. I picked it up, and started wondering who this person was, and why he had deer horns.

$\mathcal{I}$ REMEMBER how my great-uncle Jerry would sit on the porch and whittle all day long. Once he whittled me a toy boat out of a larger toy boat I had. It was almost as good as the first one, except now it had bumpy whittle marks all over it. And no paint, because he had whittled off the paint.

𝓗ERE'S A good thing to do if you go to a party and you don't know anybody: First, take out the garbage. Then go around and collect any extra garbage that people might have, like a crumpled-up napkin, and take that out too. Pretty soon people will want to meet the busy garbage guy.

$\mathcal{S}$OMETIMES I think you have to march right in and demand your rights, even if you don't know what your rights are, or who the person is you're talking to. Then, on the way out, slam the door.

*I*F YOU'RE A cowboy, and you're dragging a guy behind your horse, I bet it would really make you mad if you looked back and the guy was reading a magazine.

I THINK THAT A hat that has a little cannon that fires and then goes back inside the hat is at least a decade away.

*I*F YOUR friend is already dead, and being
eaten by vultures, I think it's okay to feed
some bits of your friend to one of the vultures,
to teach him to do some tricks. But *only* if
you're serious about adopting the vulture.

$\mathscr{B}$ROKEN promises don't upset me. I just think, why did they believe me?

$\mathcal{I}$F YOU WANT to sue somebody,
just get a little plastic skeleton
and lay it in their yard. Then tell
them their ants ate your baby.

*I*F YOU EVER crawl inside an old hollow log and go to sleep, and while you're in there some guys come and seal up both ends and then put it on a truck and take it to another city, boy, I don't know what to tell you.

CAN'T THE Marx Brothers be arrested and maybe even tortured for all the confusion and problems they've caused?

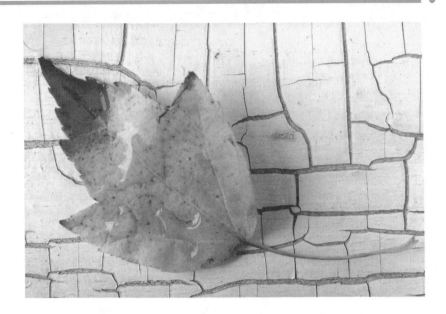

𝒴OU KNOW what's probably a good thing to hang on your porch in the summertime, to keep mosquitos away from you and your guests? Just a big bag full of blood.

I'M JUST guessing, but probably one of the early signs that your radarscope is wearing out is something I call "image fuzz-out." But I've never even seen a radarscope, so I wouldn't totally go by what I've just said here.

*S*OMETIMES I think the so-called experts actually *are* experts.

$\mathcal{O}$NE THING vampire children
have to be taught early on is,
don't run with a wooden stake.

$\mathscr{I}$F YOU GO to a costume party at your boss's house, wouldn't you think a good costume would be to dress up like the boss's wife? Trust me, it's not.

$\mathscr{M}$OST OF THE time it was probably real bad being stuck down in a dungeon. But some days, when there was a bad storm outside, you'd look out your little window and think, "Boy, I'm glad I'm not out in *that*."

$\mathcal{I}$NSTEAD OF a Seeing Eye dog, what about a gun? It's cheaper than a dog, plus if you walk around shooting all the time, people are going to get out of the way. Cars too!

$\mathscr{B}$ASICALLY, there are three ways the skunk and I are a lot alike. The first is we both like to spread our "stink" around. The second is we both get hit by cars a lot. The third is stripes.

$\mathcal{W}$HEN I WAS a child, there were times when we had to entertain ourselves. And usually the best way to do that was to turn on the TV.

$\mathcal{T}$HE FIRST thing was, I learned to forgive myself. Then I told myself, "Go ahead and do whatever you want, it's okay by me."

*C*ONSIDER THE daffodil. And while you're doing that, I'll be over here, looking through your stuff.

$\mathscr{I}$F I WAS THE head of a country that lost
a war, and I had to sign a peace treaty,
just as I was signing I'd glance over the
treaty and then suddenly act surprised.
"Wait a minute! I thought *we* won!"

*F*OR MAD scientists who keep brains in jars, here's a tip: why not add a slice of lemon to each jar, for freshness.

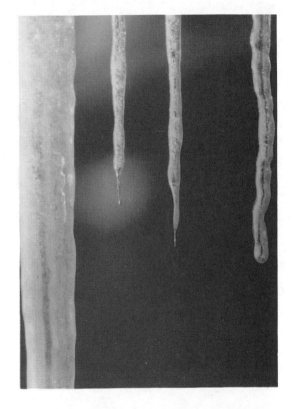

I'D LIKE TO see a nature film where an eagle swoops down and pulls a fish out of a lake, and then maybe he's flying along, low to the ground, and the fish pulls a worm out of the ground. Now *that's* a documentary!

*I*F YOU WERE an ancient barbarian, I bet a real embarrassing thing would be if you were sacking Rome and your cape got caught on something and you couldn't get it unhooked, and you had to ask another barbarian to unhook it for you.

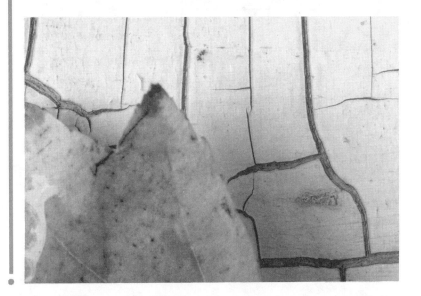

$\mathcal{S}$OMETIMES I wish Marta was more loyal to me. Like the other day. The car parked next to ours had a real dirty windshield, so I wrote THIS CAR LOOKS LIKE A FART in the dirt. Later I asked Marta if she thought it was a childish thing to do. She said, "Well, maybe." Man, whose side is she on, anyway?

*I*NSTEAD OF putting a
quarter under a kid's
pillow, how about a
pine cone? That way,
he learns that "wishing"
isn't going to save our
national forests.

$\mathcal{S}$OMETIMES you have to be careful when selecting a new nickname for yourself. For instance, let's say you have chosen the nickname "Fly Head." Normally, you would think that "Fly Head" would mean a person who has beautiful swept-back features, as if flying through the air. But think again. Couldn't it also mean "having a head like a fly"? I'm afraid some people might actually think that.

$\mathcal{W}$HEN YOU go ice-skating, try not to swing your arms too much, because that really annoys me.

$\mathcal{S}$OMEBODY told me how frightening it was how much topsoil we are losing each year, but I told that story around the campfire and nobody got scared.

I REMEMBER one day I was at Grandpa's farm and I asked him about sex. He sort of smiled and said, "Maybe instead of telling you what sex is, why don't we go out to the horse pasture and I'll show you." So we did, and there on the ground were my parents having sex.

*I*NSTEAD OF burning a guy at the stake, what about burning him at the *stilts*? It probably lasts longer, plus it moves around.

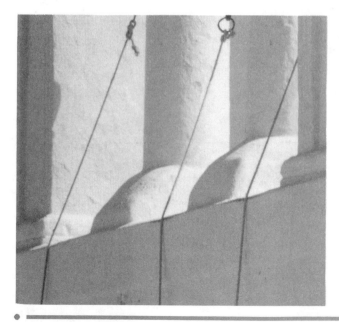

*Y*OU KNOW what would be the most terrifying
thing that could ever happen to a flea?
Getting caught inside a watch somehow.
You don't even care, do you.

I HOPE THAT after I die, people will say of me: "That guy sure owed me a lot of money."

*I*F YOU SEE an animal and you can't tell if it's a skunk or a cat, here's a good saying to help: "Black and white, stinks all right. Tabby-colored, likes a fella."

I BET THE sparrow looks at the parrot and thinks, yes, you can talk, but *listen to yourself*!

*W*HEN THIS girl at the museum asked me whom I liked better, Monet or Manet, I said, "I like mayonnaise." She just stared at me, so I said it again, louder. Then she left. I guess she went to try to find some mayonnaise for me.

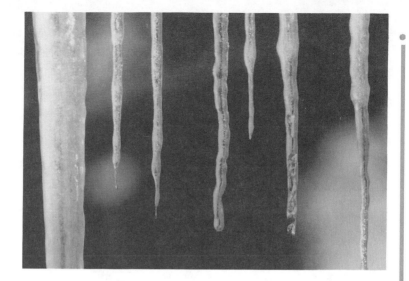

$\mathscr{M}$ANY PEOPLE do not realize that the snowshoe can be used for a great many things besides walking on snow. For instance, it can be used to carry pancakes from the stove to the breakfast table. Also, it can be used to carry uneaten pancakes from the table to the garbage. Finally, it can be used as a kind of strainer, where you force pancakes through the strings to see if a piece of gold got in a pancake somehow.

*H*IGHER beings from outer space may not want to tell us the secrets of life, because we're not ready. But maybe they'll change their tune after a little torture.

$\mathscr{A}$DVICE TO vampires: why not "do your business" as a bat, not a human. Easier that way, and less pollution.

*A*s THE SNOW started to fall, he tugged his coat tighter around himself. Too tight, as it turned out.

"This is the fourth coat crushing this year," said the police sergeant as he outlined the body with a special pencil that writes on snow.

I'D LIKE TO see a guy tap-dancing so fast his legs actually broke, because it would finally establish a "tap barrier," and we could move on from there.

*L*ET'S BE honest:
isn't a lot of what
we call tap-dancing
really just nerves?

A FUNNY thing is if you're out hiking and your friend gets bitten by a poisonous snake, tell him you're going for help, then go about ten feet and pretend *you* got bit by a snake. Then start an argument about who's going to go get help. A lot of guys will start crying. That's why it makes you feel good when you tell them it was just a joke.

$\mathcal{T}$HE OTHER day I got out my can opener and was opening a can of worms when I thought, "What am I doing?!"

$\mathcal{I}$F YOU WEAR a toupee, why not let your friends try it on for a while. Come on, we're not going to hurt it.

$\mathscr{I}$ GUESS one of the funniest memories of my grandfather was the time I was at his house and that tied-up man with the gag in his mouth came hopping out of the closet and started yelling that *he* was really my grandfather and the other guy was an impostor and to run for help. Who was that guy?! Oh, well, never saw *him* again.

THE TIRED and thirsty prospector threw himself down at the edge of the watering hole and started to drink. But then he looked around and saw skulls and bones everywhere. Uh-oh, he thought. This watering hole is reserved for skeletons.

$\mathscr{I}$'M TELLING you, just attach a big parachute *to the plane itself*! Is anyone listening to me?!

$\mathcal{I}$ THINK THERE probably should be a rule that if you're talking about how many loaves of bread a bullet will go through, it's understood that you mean lengthwise loaves. Otherwise it makes no sense.

*I*T'S FUNNY that pirates were always going around searching for treasure, and they never realized that the real treasure was the fond memories they were creating.

*I*F YOU GET invited to your first orgy, don't just show up nude. That's a common mistake. You have to let nudity "happen."

I THINK A good scene in a movie would be where one scientist tells another scientist: "You know what will save the world? You're holding it in your hand." And the other scientist looks, and in his hand are some peanuts. Then, when he looks up, the first scientist is being taken away to the insane asylum.

$\mathcal{O}$NE THING a computer can do that most humans can't is be sealed up in a cardboard box and sit in a warehouse.

$\mathcal{I}$F SOMEONE told me it wasn't "fashionable" to talk about freedom, I think I'd just have to look him square in the eye and say, "Okay, *you tell me* what's 'fashionable.'" But he won't. And you know why? Because you can't ask someone what's fashionable in a smart-alecky way like that. You have to be friendly and say, "By the way, what's fashionable?"

$\mathcal{W}$HEN YOU go to a party at somebody's house, don't automatically assume that the drinks are free. Ask, and ask often.

*I*F I EVER become a mummy, I'm going to have it so when somebody opens my lid a boxing glove on a spring shoots out.

I THINK A good product would be "Baby Duck Hat." It's a fake baby duck, which you strap on top of your head. Then you go swimming underwater until you find a mommy duck and her babies, and you join them. Then, all of a sudden, you stand up out of the water and roar like Godzilla. Man, those ducks really take off!

Also, Baby Duck Hat is good for parties.

I WISH I HAD a dollar for every time I spent a dollar, because then, yahoo!, I'd have all my money back.

*𝒴*OU KNOW what makes good hair for a snowman? *Real* hair. Don't ask me why, but it works.

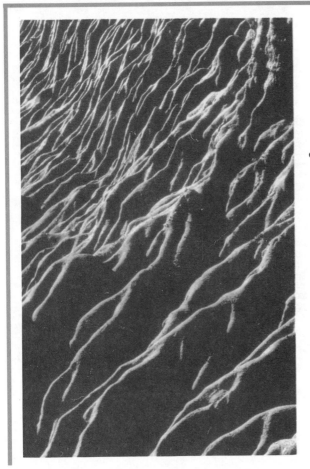

*I*F THE CAPTAIN invited me to his party, after he had whipped me earlier in the day up on deck, I guess I'd go, but I'd try to find some excuse to leave early.

*I*SN'T IT FUNNY how one minute life can be such a struggle, and the next minute you're just driving real fast, swerving back and forth across the road?

ONE WAY I think you can tell if you have a curse on you is if you open a box of toothpicks and they all fly up and stick in your face.

$\mathscr{T}$HE TIGER can't change his spots. No, wait, he did! Good for him!

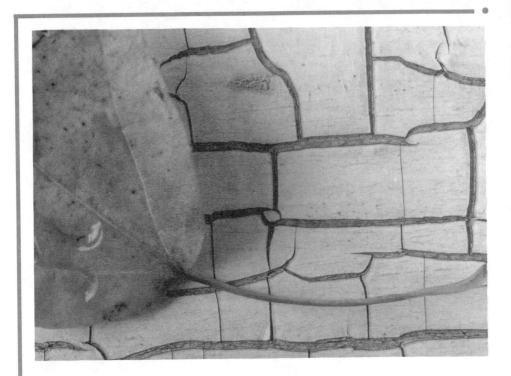

I THINK MY favorite monster movie is *Gone With the Wind*, because it has that ear monster and that big-dress monster.

I GUESS I kinda lost control, because in the middle of the play I ran up and lit the evil puppet villain on fire.

No, I didn't. Just kidding. I just said that to illustrate one of the human emotions, which is freaking out. Another emotion is greed, as when someone kills someone for money, or something like that. Another emotion is generosity, as when you pay someone double what he paid for his stupid puppet.

$\mathcal{H}$ERE'S A good tip for when you go to the beach: a sand dollar may look like a nice cracker that someone left, but trust me, they don't taste like it.

$\mathcal{I}$ BET WHEN they weren't fighting, Vikings with horn helmets had to stick potatoes on the ends of the horns, so as to avoid eye-pokings to fellow Vikings and lady Vikings.

$\mathcal{H}$ERE'S A suggestion for a
new animal, if some new
ones get created or evolve:
something that stings you,
then laughs at you.

*I*F YOU WERE a pirate, you know what would be the one thing that would really make you mad? Treasure chests with no handles. How the hell are you supposed to carry it?!

$\mathcal{D}$ON'T EVER get your speedometer confused with your clock, like I did once, because the faster you go the later you think you are.

You KNOW how to paint a room real fast? Just put paint rollers on your feet and somehow figure out how to skate up the walls and across the ceiling.

I THINK A CUTE movie idea would be about a parrot who is raised by eagles. It would be cute because the parrot can't seem to act like an eagle. After a while, though, to keep the movie from getting boring, maybe put in some pornography. Later, we see the happy parrot flying along, acting like an eagle. He sees two parrots below and starts to attack, but it's his parents. Then, some more pornography.

$\mathcal{I}$ GUESS THE hard thing for a lot of people to accept is why God would allow me to go running through their yards, yelling and spinning around.

$\mathcal{I}$F I LIVED back in the olden days, and the doctor put leeches on me, I'd tell him to put them on my face, in the shape of a beard, so I could see how I'd look.

$\mathcal{I}$F I COULD be any kind of dog, I think I'd be one of those little yappy dogs, because while you're sitting there on the couch trying to sound real smart, I'm just sitting there, yapping away. Just yappin' and yappin', and there's nothing you can do about it, because I live here.

$\mathcal{I}$F I WAS A cowboy in a lynch mob, I think I'd try to stay near the back. That way, if somebody shamed us into disbanding, I could sort of slip off to the side and pretend I was window-shopping or something.

𝒟o you know what happens when you slice
a golf ball in half? Someone gets mad at you.
I found this out the hard way.

ONE THING about my aunt Nadie: she was gruff on the outside, but if you ever needed something, like a spanking or a scolding, she'd give it to you.

$\mathscr{I}$T'S INTERESTING to think that my ancestors used to live in the trees, like apes, until finally they got the nerve to head out onto the plains, where some were probably hit by cars.

I DON'T SAY that the bird is "good" or the bat is "bad." But I will say this: at least the bird is less nude.

*I*F YOU MAKE ships in a bottle, I bet the thing that really makes your heart sink is when you look in and there at the wheel is Captain Termite.

$\mathcal{I}$ DON'T PRETEND to have all the answers. I don't pretend to even know what the questions are. Hey, where am I?